After the Flowers

After the Flowers

Life Beyond Widowhood

ALICE GROSSMAN DANIELS

FITHIAN PRESS, SANTA BARBARA, 1996

Gratitude to the following people, who were invaluable to me in the writing of this book: Bob Marks, Sander Allen, Arthur Orduna, Kay Myers, Rita Nathanson, and to all the friends who kept me on high whenever they could... you know who you are.

Published by Fithian Press
A division of Daniel and Daniel, Publishers, Inc.
Post Office Box 1525
Santa Barbara, CA 93102

Design by Eric Larson

Daniels, Alice Grossman, date
    After the flowers / Alice Grossman Daniels.
        p.   cm.
        ISBN 1-56474-173-7 (pbk. : alk. paper)
        1. Daniels, Alice Grossman, date   . 2. Widows--United States--
Case studies. 3. Widowhood--United States--Case studies.
    I. Title.
    HQ1058.5.U5D35   1996
    305.48'654--dc20
                                                96-5262
                                                CIP

My loving appreciation to daughter Suse and her wonderful husband, Mark, for their loving support.

Contents

Be It Ever So Humble

Images

Dollars and Sense

The Crowd Around Me

Widows and Widowers

Odds 'n' Ends

Epilogue

After the Flowers

Prologue

In the Beginning

In one of my more emotional moments, I called my friend for a shoulder to lean on. He listened, as he usually did, and then said, "Alice, have you ever thought of writing down your thoughts in a diary? I've heard this can give cathartic relief." I figured, "What could it hurt?" and started to do just that. When next we talked, he asked if I had taken his advice. I had to tell him that I had started writing, but some of the stuff was coming out funny, and it didn't seem respectful somehow. The advertising man in him must have taken over. He chuckled and said, "Keep writing!" And so I did.

Shades of Black

And the Beat Goes On

During the services, I sit in the room the funeral home delegates to the family, amazingly clear-headed, with my daughter's arm around me. I become intrigued as the eulogy compares Dick to the product he manufactured, the Ross Root Feeder. "Dick nourished his family, friends and business associates from the roots, and they all flourished under his guidance." My youngest son leans over and says, "Gee, Mom, had we but known, we could have had memorial Root Feeders for sale in the lobby." I grin and think, "And the beat goes on." I remember Dick making wisecracks like that during his father's funeral. Life does and must go on.

Always the Hostess

With our friends coming and going before and after the funeral, I remember being relieved that I didn't have to worry about what to serve them. There's always a silver lining.

Son of a Gun

I want to tell you about Dick. I must write about him in depth, but when I start to frame my thoughts, it hurts too much. So for now just know that he was a son of a gun to live with—but he was my son of a gun.

A Special Brother

My doctor brother-in-law was in town at the end, although we didn't realize it was the end. He sized up Dick's situation immediately; he felt he was just slipping away. Though he was staying at his mother's, he spent many hours with us during those last few days. He encouraged me to get out of the house with my friends, because he could see that after the last couple of hard years, my steel was starting to melt. We seemed to form a bond, and in the end our unspoken goal was accomplished. My husband died a peaceful death, not the kind associated with cancer. Afterwards, and during the last fifteen months, my brother-in-law became a wonderful friend and listener. He calls me every two weeks and sincerely looks out for what he calls his "teenage sister." He has become a friend, not family. His behavior has been one of the exceptions, not the rule, in that family.

Food Heals Some Wounds

I realize now that my friends saw the end coming before I did. They swooped into my home with every kind of meal imaginable. Bless them, they stayed for days afterwards, feeding the world who came to pay respects. When the fruit baskets and meat platters started to arrive, I kidded about writing a book, "The Revenge of the Meat Platter." This was a bit prophetic, considering I never dreamed at the time that I would ever be writing anything, except possibly over seven hundred "Thank You" notes. I still can't look at meat platters.

Girlfriends

My close friends in town did not step forth until they sensed that the end was near, which turned out to be a couple of days before Dick died. No matter how bad the sick days were, I knew if I called them they would insist on coming over. Other than having someone to talk to, I didn't want to dwell on the situation. I really was quite content to just put an imaginary bubble around the two of us, and in that way keep the rest of the world out. When the ambulance finally came to take Dick to the hospital, two very special friends were upstairs with me, their arms holding me tight. I just couldn't stand the thought of seeing my darling leaving his home for what I knew would be the last time. Afterwards, one of these gals took me in her car to follow him to the hospital, where she stayed glued to me all evening until just before the end. The outpouring of affection was awesome, and more than one out-of-town relative remarked that the generosity of food and spirit was extraordinary. But it didn't stop there. It seemed that everyone wanted to get in on the act; old friends and new joined my regular crowd to offer lunch dates, funny cards in the mail, invitations to family dinners, as well as parties galore, after a suitable interval. Then there were the husbands. Dick being the first in the crowd to die made it hard for some to look me in the eye. But they still were there to offer support whenever they could. For someone like me, who felt she had been kicked into another world, these loving gestures more than helped to bring me back. I thank the heavens for my family of friends, and for the "girlfriends" who make it all possible.

Real Men Can Cry

Later I would remember my friend suggesting I "stop with all the hugging" of the husbands. He went on to explain that that would be a good way to lose their wives as friends. I told him Dick's men friends needed support after the funeral, in some cases, even more than I did. More than once I found myself following someone out of my house of crowds to offer a shoulder to one of them who did not want to break down in public. He was their friend, and his death also threatened their own mortality. Real men can cry!

Role Models

It's hard to know how to be a proper widow when you don't have any role models to emulate. I kept feeling that I had to be in charge of all events relating to the funeral, because I knew what Dick would have wanted (although we never really discussed it). Above all, he would have hated the thought that his loved ones were tearing themselves apart over his passing. Even today I can imagine him saying, "It's no big deal!" This was an understatement, of course, but that's the kind of man he was. I found myself directing traffic as best I could, to the amazement of his family and my sons, who kept waiting for me to ask for help. I couldn't afford that luxury because (right or wrong) I knew that if I did, they would bungle the job, and I couldn't, or wouldn't, allow that to happen. I was so busy that I can't remember at what point it was that I started to feel self-conscious. I began to realize how uncomfortable everyone was, and wondered what I could do to get them to relax. I worried that my "smooth" attitude seemed somehow disrespectful to Dick's memory. Was I looking and acting as a bereaved widow should? Suddenly I remembered how well Jackie Kennedy handled everything at her husband's funeral. So she became my role model of sorts. Now how's that for pomposity? Surprisingly enough, though, that seemed to get me through some tough moments, including the funeral itself. My only relief from all this playacting was to go to my room to be alone, to sleep or cry. It felt so good to feel the tears flow. No hysterics—I had been through too much for that—just soft flowing tears. Then I would get up, go downstairs and start all over again. Needless to say, when the days of crowds were over, it was nice to let my hair down. Do all widows have to do this, or is it just people like me, who feel "no one can do it like you"? Looking back, in all due modesty, I feel it was a hard act to follow. Dick would have been proud.

Band-Aids

It still seems a little crazy that sympathetic friends kept urging me to get new clothes. It was like putting Band-Aids on an open wound. However, trying to keep the days busy between visits to the lawyer, I would follow their advice, and pretty soon practice made perfect. Fancy new duds really do have therapeutic qualities.

Three Wonderful Children

I talk to my daughter in Kansas City at least once a day. If I'm really lucky, I talk to my sons, who live in town, maybe once a month. I keep remembering the old saying, "A son's a son 'til he takes a wife, a daughter's a daughter

23

all her life." So what else is new!

Rabbi–Priest Joke

As luck would have it, our rabbi was in Israel when Dick died, and our temple was in the hands of a most capable young rabbi-in-training, Rabbi Suzanne. A few hours after the funeral she came back to the house to hold a small service for close family and friends. Shortly afterwards the door opened and Father Jim walked in to pay his respects. This handsome young priest was a friend of the family and wanted to be with us at this time. The first thing that entered my mind, I said, "Father, have I got a girl for you!" Needless to say, my fellow mourners who overheard this conversation almost dropped dead themselves. But this darling man followed me into the family room mumbling, "Aunt Alice, you're a bad lady." I made the introductions and then left them alone. A few minutes later daughter Suse told me, "Mom, it's like a rabbi–priest joke, where the rabbi and the priest are sitting on a love seat in a house of mourning, just gabbing away." About five minutes later, Father Jim came to tell me what a nice girl she was. Shortly after that, a slightly flushed rabbi put her hands on my shoulder (she looked like she would have preferred them around my neck) and said, "Very funny!" I know that Dick would have thought so.... I did. Months later, I received a note from her, wanting to know how I was doing and also telling me that whenever she's at a gathering, ecumenical in nature, she always repeats this story, and usually brings down the house. Looking back, I guess I could always say, "The Devil made me do it." But I have a hunch it just might have been the newest angel that spurred me on.

The Patient

It was hard having my first check-up after Dick died. One of the reasons was that the office was located in the same building where I had spent all too many hours with him at his doctor's office. In the elevator I noticed a woman staring at me. She finally said, "You may not remember me, but I used to notice you last year at the doctor's office with your husband. It's a relief seeing you look so much better." She seemed so surprised when I told her I had not been the patient, and that my husband had passed away. I guess I didn't want to compound the issue by asking her whether she herself was the patient, or her mate. This experience tended to remind me what I had learned the hard way, that is, how fatal diseases affect the family as well as the afflicted. Yuk!

Check-Ups

I've always been apprehensive about check-ups, but now, being alone, there is even more reason to be frightened. When and if the time ever comes that the doctors have bad news for me, who will be there for me? It's just not fair! Dick had me; now I have no one.

"W" is Better than "D"

I have always thought that in divorce, the human factor is involved in the decision-making, whereas in death a life has been ripped from two people, not one. So in this respect, widowhood does have that element of respect that divorce, no matter who's at fault, doesn't carry. But when my daughter needed business advice in the beginning, I would have gladly sacrificed the honors to have a father for her to turn to, bitter feelings be damned. A divorced friend of mine told me she was struck by the inequity of all the attention offered to me, when she felt lucky to get one or two phone calls of concern after her divorce. When you think of it, it's really not fair. I guess in this way "W" is better than "D," but alone is alone is alone.

Promises, Promises

My husband lied to me. He promised fortune hunters, re-marriage in six months and his family always at my side. I promised him at the time, wryly, that I would watch out for Greek gods bearing gifts, as well as investment opportunities that seemed too good to be true. Come to think of it, where are these creeps now? I would welcome the attention. Eighteen months later, the idea of sharing in a marriage or relationship tends to tickle my funny bone. Someone should have grabbed me when all this was new and I felt like half a person without a man. The family was at loose ends. They had also lost their leader. So with the help of very special friends, I had to become my own.

What's in a Name?

Even right after the funeral, when I would think out loud and say slowly, "I am a widow," close friends would cry, "Don't say that—you're an Alice." Now pals tease me by calling me the "Widder Daniels." I think I'm going to stick with the term "widow" for a while, because if I should ever start thinking of myself as "single," then I might be tempted to also take off my ring. Then I really would be alone. Maybe "Alice" would be better in the long run.

You Were a Good, Submissive Wife

Now that's a back-handed compliment if I ever heard one. This comment came from a very well-meaning friend (a non-practicing psychologist). At first I was a little upset with her observation; but reflecting on it later, I realized that of course I was submissive. That's the only way someone married in the early fifties, at just twenty years old, could be. Furthermore, it worked, because in thirty-five years (short two weeks) of marriage, it was so much easier that way. After all, someone always has to be on top, and it's usually the husband. Now that's food for thought for yet another subject. Hmmmm!

Red Licorice and Solitaire

After a week of crowds at the house, the calls and invitations started. Three days after the funeral I decided it was time to experience at least two evenings alone. I refused invitations, did some shopping, and settled in waiting for the pain. I figured it was time, and I was strong enough to face the inevitable alone. About an hour later the phone rang, and one of my friends asked what I was doing. I explained that I had picked up a deck of cards for solitaire, a package of red licorice and jug of bottled water. I was now in the widow business. After a couple of shocked giggles, I got off the phone and wondered how I could hurt so much and still be such a wise guy. After two nights of being alone, I decided I had inflicted enough punishment on myself in exile, and I was ready to face the world again. I haven't eaten red licorice or played solitaire for at least three years now. It still hurts too much.

The Soaps

"Just don't hang around watching soap operas; you've lived them. You don't need reruns." These words were in a letter I received three months after the funeral. Obviously it was a directive telling me that it was time to get off the rocking chair and get involved in volunteer work, seek a new career or, most emphatically, begin to live again. What my friend didn't realize was that my two favorite soaps had become, and still are, old friends of mine. From the time Dick had his first surgery until now, my sleeping habits have been very erratic. As a matter of fact, so were his, because we used to meet each other at the top of the stairs each night. I decided to tape my favorite soaps (I'll never tell which ones) to watch in the late evening or when I got up during the night. Even now, when I have time to watch during the day, I always save them for later. It's become a habit, and I suppose when I stop it, I'll know I'm healed, or at least as healed as I'm going to be. But in the meantime it's a comfort, something to look forward to, and at the very least, a reward or treat (I believe the term is behavior modification) for getting through yet another day. But don't tell him I'm still watching.

We'll Always Be There for You

It's amazing, looking back, how friends turned into family, and some family turned into distant friends. Very distant. More like Xmas card acquaintances...without the cards.

It's Not So Bad

In the beginning, men friends who had lost their wives would comfort me (when they learned of Dick's illness) by saying, "It's not so bad." Dick and I used to laugh about this, because they had in most cases been celibate for at least two months afterwards. Also, look at all the casseroles they got. I just heard of another name for the women who pursue them. They're now called the "Brisket Brigade" in some circles. It just doesn't work that way for widows. Damn!

Single Shopping

It was not as hard to get used to shopping for one as it might be for others in my situation. After a lifetime of being married to a traveling man, I was familiar with eating alone, at home and away. However, after the "sick years," when the cupboards and freezer were always filled with comfort foods (potato chips, sour cream dips, ice cream bars and loads of Milky Ways to be frozen) to make me feel better, it was time to get back to normal eating. Lean Cuisine-type meals made meal planning easy. Not interesting, just easy.

Ours, Mine, etc.

Never having been at a loss for words (or could you tell), I found myself stumbling around when I would talk about "our" friends. It was a habit hard to break. I would find myself saying things like "C'mon over to our house—I mean mine." Realizing that this must be normal for one who's been part of a pair for almost a lifetime, I wonder now at what point I stopped stumbling.

Family Specials

Some Things My Mother Taught Me

Although we were not rich, my Jewish mother was overly wealthy in the basic common sense that she shared with her family. A few of her directives come back to me, especially now that I find myself newly single and more than a little insecure about many aspects of this situation.

"When you don't know what they're talking about, keep your mouth shut.... They'll never know for sure."

"Always be with people that you can learn from; they don't have to be Ph.D.s, but they should be able to do something well, even if it's only a cheesecake."

"Your best friends won't tell you, only a mother cares!"

"When it comes to boyfriends, you have no girlfriends."

It's still hard to believe that I haven't been able to talk to her for a least four years. She's been in a semi-coma with Alzheimer's disease for the last year and a half. During Dick's illness, I couldn't leave to visit her in California. Even though she has my dad and brother there, I live with guilt. Now that I'm free to be with her, it serves no real purpose. But I do go to be with Dad.

After growing up seventy to eighty years ago on Delancy Street in New York, Mom was determined that her own two children would be the sharpest kids on the Chicago block where we were raised. She was four feet, eleven inches at the top. I thought of her as "little Napoleon" because she ruled the roost. I always teased her that she liked my brother best because he became a top-notch physician, and I was just a mother hen. But when she would look at me, the joy and pride that I saw in her eyes would bring tears to mine. She always needled me "for your own good," even to the end, and my three children could never understand why I would get upset when she didn't approve of a latest outfit or hair style. In spite of it all, I was proud to pass on all that I had learned (for better or worse) to my children. She had a saying for that too: "Someday you'll have children just like you, and then...." Bless her heart! And then there's Dad!

And Then There's Dad

I'm helping Dad with a tray in one of the new buffet restaurants during a visit to California. One of the waitresses behind the counter asks, "Is that your husband?" I try not to show my surprise, but he just chuckles and moves on. What a blow. When we're sitting down, I ask, "Aren't you flattered to be seen with such a cute young chick?" He looks up with a twinkle in his eye, but continues eating. After a pregnant pause I tease, "Wait a minute, are you implying I'm too old for you?" He leans over and smiles, "You said it, dear, I didn't."

May I present my wonderful ninety-two-year-old father, whose cup is always half full. He was the baby of his family, born in this country to a rabbi's daughter and to a professor of Latin and German at U.C.L.A. who later became one of the first Reform rabbis in this country. Dad's illustrious older brother was a very important part of the U.S. Steel executive force, a prominent author of text relating to metallurgy and a participant in the Manhattan Project. I'm told that when he died forty years ago, someone flew down from the White House to disconnect his phone. His very special sister was also prominent as a director of social services in New York City and Denver. Dad never quite made the Golden Circle, but was able to support his own family by working for forty years in one of the offices of U.S. Steel. While Mother was the fire that kept things going, my dad, almost always taking a back seat, was the one with the sensitivity for me to draw on. I can still see him kissing the long braids that Mom had just cut off twelve-year-old me. It seems ironic that it was only in the past years that we became really close. He was busy caretaking Mom, until he could do no more, while I was doing the same with Dick. Although thousands of miles apart, our frequent phone calls gave us courage to do what we had to do. Though the last few years have proven I must have inherited a good share of my mother's strength, the surfacing of all my sensitivities just had to come from Dad.

If You Knew Suse

After two sons, it was thrilling to finally have a daughter. (She dropped the "i" from Susie, but no one's perfect.) Little did I know at the time that decades later I would be estranged from my sons, and she would be, to me, my only child of record. Because of the circumstances, we have become more than just family, and many times we take turns playing "Mommie." She's very protective, and considering my relationship with the rest of the family, it's quite a blessing. From before her father's illness until now, our arms have always been around each other for comfort, in person or via long distance from Kansas City, where she now lives. She has a darling new boyfriend, who also keeps an eye on me, and it hurts me that Dick never met him, because he too would have adored the guy. I see her growing into a lovely, bright, self-assured young lady. I could write reams, but trust me, if you knew Suse, you'd understand.

Sweep It Under the Rug

It's been fourteen years now that Ursula has been with me for the purpose of cleaning my home. I use the word purpose lightly, because she has also become a friend and confidant in the deepest sense of the word. In the befores, I used to tease Dick that if ever there was a choice between them, Ursula would win hands down. Then he would chuckle and write in the dust that she had inadvertently overlooked, "Alice loves Dick." He'd then wait to see how long it would be until either one of us would notice. Two years before the illness, our company had gone through some serious financial reversals, and at one point I had to tell her that her days with us were numbered. She answered, "You're not getting rid of me that easy. Forget the money!" Thank goodness it wasn't necessary, but I'll never forget her kindness. She wants my writing to bring me great success, because "I'll be behind you wherever you go, schlepping the bags." Her husband will be thrilled! This shy German war bride has turned into a super-sharp gal with lots of savvy, and her encouragement and feisty spirit have been invaluable to me in my recovery. But don't try to steal her; she's mine! About the stuff concerning her housekeeping talents...well, let's just follow her lead and sweep it under the rug.

Be It Ever So Humble

Hausfrau

It's the weirdest thing in the world.... Now that I'm single I'm acting more like a wife. Lately I find myself browsing in stores for home furnishings rather than clothes (well, not all the time), wanting to keep everything neat and pretty just for me. Now that I'm in the process of redecorating, I'm feeling comforted with all the soft sherbet colors that are surrounding me. Dick would have flipped, because he was always leaning on me to take more interest in the house. In fact, he kept saying that I was going to let everything go to hell after he was gone. Then why the surge of pride when I look around me, and why did it take widowhood to cultivate this nesting influence? It's a puzzlement!

A Selfish Thought

What's happening? Now I'm getting a wild desire to plant pretty flowers, lots of pretty flowers, in my backyard. How can I do this to Dick's memory; he always wanted me to, and I was never interested. Up until eight or nine months ago, the memories of the overabundance of floral arrangements after Dick's surgeries and the funeral turned me off to flowers of any kind. It got to the point that it was hard to even walk into a florist shop. It was just too upsetting. Then gradually I started to pick up a few posies at a time for dinner parties. The other day a lovely neighbor brought over an exquisite purple iris that I've been staring at on my kitchen table. I keep trying to fight these urges, and I have a crazy thought that if I don't plant them at his grave, he won't know. At this point, the main thing that's holding me back is that the selfishness of self-indulgence would make me feel too guilty to enjoy them in the first place.

Maybe I'll just have to ask my neighbor for another.

The Naturalist

Now I have a bird feeder on my deck, and I'm getting so much enjoyment watching the birds it attracts. First flowers and now this. How ironic that only now am I turning into the naturalist that Dick always wanted me to be.

What's Cooking?

Somehow I feel that this might be an opportunity to write about the challenges of cooking for one. Yes, there is a life besides Lean Cuisine, and it doesn't have to be difficult—you just have to be hungry enough.

That's Entertainment

They say it's normal for widows to gradually be excluded from the guest lists of their married friends. This is not done intentionally, but it still hurts. They just weren't lucky enough to have a perennial bachelor for an advisor...and advise he did, right from the start. If it were up to him, I would have had a huge bash two weeks after the funeral. I had to remind him that I had just had a houseful, the hard way. It took me about six months to get up my nerve, but then I started with an informal Sunday night supper for "our" dinner group, which had been going strong for about twenty-five years. It was strange for me, but even more uncomfortable for my guests to see me hostessing without my host. But this was a temporary situation, and soon they became involved in helping, with the guys tending bar and the gals helping out in the kitchen. I guess they realized that if I could try, well, they could do no less. The evening was not a barrel of laughs, as you can imagine, but it was nevertheless filled with nostalgia about their dear friend, and that in itself brought some laughter, even with tears in our eyes. This experience reminded me that being single is no excuse for being inhospitable. Sunday night is great for entertaining because no one likes to cook then anyway. I have been doing this kind of stuff, one way or another, ever since, though my friend still keeps nagging me to do more. What does he care? Living out of town, he doesn't have to eat what I cook.

Cookies

I'm baking homemade chocolate chip cookies for a party. That is unusual because I haven't baked anything from scratch for years. In fact, a lifetime ago, when my children would see me baking in the kitchen, they would ask, "Who died, Mommy?" One would have thought this urge would have been better served when Dick was so ill, because maybe it would have helped to cheer him up. I try to convince myself that I did everything I could for him during the hard days, but I keep dwelling on what I forgot to do. The whole thing's ridiculous. It's over, and all the cookies in the world won't bring him back. But I'm so tired of these guilt trips!

Wonderful Things

It was one-thirty in the morning, and I was stripping off old kitchen wallpaper to get ready for the new. I was both humming and thinking "If Dick could see me now," because he never trusted me with such chores. Suddenly a childhood poem came to mind. "The world is so full of such wonderful things, I'm sure we should all be as happy as kings." The next morning I would recall that Robert Louis Stevenson was the author, but at that moment, standing with paper peelings all around me, I realized that for all practical purposes, the heavy part of mourning was over. It had been fifteen months.

Sensitivities

I've almost finished redoing my home, and now it's really "mine," not "ours." Beautiful limited editions are starting to line my walls, and because I purchased a little CD player, beautiful music resounds throughout. My sensitivities have been aroused and somehow satisfied. I would hate to think that I had to lose a husband to reach this state...but how sweet it is.

Images

Alice Through the Looking Glass

Every so often I look through a figurative looking glass to check on the changes within me. I see more and more the poised single woman looking back. The problem is that the Alice that is asking for inward reflection is a composite of the conventional housewife and mother. Somehow I can't convince my psyche that I'm no longer the same, and I wonder what it will take for the inner me to catch up with reality. I never felt like this before. But then again, maybe I never took the time to notice.

Humorless

"Don't lose your sense of humor," my friend told me recently. I was in doubt as to how to handle a sticky situation. I realized maybe his warning was too late. With the growing confidence I have in myself now, both as a human being and as a capable single in today's world, I find myself increasingly serious, nervous and definitely less humorous. Maybe my friend the psychologist was right when she suggested that my sometimes caustic manner and brash humor were in reality a cover-up for some surprising insecurities that I brought from marriage to widowhood. I want to be funny and lighthearted again. It always gave me such a happy outlook on life...and life can certainly use it.

Fabulous

Losing weight and coloring my hair have all my friends saying I look fabulous. I guess I'm as good as I'm gonna be, but I'm still not a five-foot-nine lanky blonde. And five-foot-one with brown hair just won't do it in today's market.

Real Person

My friend grudgingly admits that I just might be turning into a real person, and not only that, someone that he could possibly admire. "That's almost a compliment. Does that mean you don't like me anymore?" This brings a pause followed by a nervous giggle. Gotcha!

Untouched

Although I've never been a particularly "touchy" person, I long for the days when I took Dick's arm around me for granted, or even his hand on mine. I guess I've come to terms with the thought that maybe there will never be another man in my life, but I do miss affectionate gestures. I feel so untouched lately, so sterile. Somehow the hugging and kissing of friends in greeting just doesn't do it. Maybe like sex itself, I'm making a big deal about something that never was a big deal. Maybe....

Medals

Taking off my rings has given me a lot of food for thought. It suddenly occurred to me that no matter what some friends have been telling me regarding the fact that Dick was pretty tough on me at times, it's only their opinion. I understood the pressures he was under, and what's more, if

I had to do it all over again, I would probably do it the same way. I really don't deserve a medal for this, because it was the only way I knew how to be a good wife, and I was. To carry this thought one step further, friends who have been so fabulous to me ever since, well, they don't deserve medals either, because I am a good person as well as a good friend. And they know that I will always be there for them when and if they need me. In fact, just maybe I didn't understand the full meaning of the word friendship before, or I wouldn't have felt so awed by the attention. What a helluva process to go through just to learn that you're okay.

Dreams

It seems funny now, but in my other life, Dick could never understand why I never had any goals or dreams. "Things just fall in my lap," I'd say, and they usually did. But now as a single, with my writings to spur me on, wonderful daydreams help pass the lonely hours. My favorite is being so successful that I have three penthouses: Park Avenue in New York, Lake Shore Drive in Chicago and one in Beverly Hills. Add to that twin villas in Florence, Italy, for my writer's hideaway, and who knows what else. But then at my age, if you're gonna dream...then dream.

Power of Presence

During a recent phone conversation with my wonderful friend and advisor, he remarked that my new columns must be giving me great power. "Power!" I answer back. "I'm not exactly in the *New York Times*." The only difference I see is that people are starting to seek me out in crowds, and I never feel like a fifth wheel at tables of couples. He retorts, "Well, maybe I should have said your celebrity status has given you the power of presence that enables you to feel complete in any situation." See why I adore the guy? He always gives me something to "think" about.

Bachelor

Thinking out loud to a dear friend, I commented that I feel happiest when I can go to affairs alone, under my own steam. I hate icy streets and evening parties where driving and parking are a problem, because then I have to depend on others to get me there. I eat out alone many evenings, so it's sometimes hard to dine with friends. I find myself ready to leave when I'm ready to leave, and it's rather insulting to dinner companions when I rush them like this. My evenings are still lonely, but the instances of going crazy are getting fewer, and the fact that the phone is often too quiet bothers me even less. I enjoy being in charge of my own destiny, and so I'm finding that solitude gives me the opportunity to think things out quietly. Maybe I've always been a loner, or I wouldn't have adapted to this life so easily. The fact that I'm addicted to lovely people in my life seems to contradict this theory. My friend has been listening patiently to my rambling. And then replies, "Do you know you're beginning to sound like your pal in Chicago, the real bachelor?" Bachelor, huh! I'm not so sure I'm ready for the status that word implies. Like I'm over the hill or something. No, I'd better start changing my ways again. Feeling definite about anything right now might take the adventure out of living...and I don't want to miss a trick.

The Guys

I decided at the very beginning that this is one widow who wouldn't be relegated to a lifetime of single women. That's where society usually puts us, you know. While I have the dearest of female friends, most of them are married. What made the difference in my case were the few fabulous men who've helped and encouraged me in this new lifestyle. These are the ones I choose to listen to, and I recognize that some of it is because Dick was a very strong-minded male, and now that I don't have my sons to lean on, these men have become very important to me. There is still nothing like hearing a male voice at the other end of a phone call. So it was a startling revelation to suddenly realize that men were for the most part the designers of my new way of life. One would think that they would want to see me in a sheltered environment, in the kitchen or participating in some form of club work. But that hasn't been the case. Instead I was encouraged to entertain, write, travel alone (if that was what I wanted) and even to feel good about being a little egocentric. They're marvelous pals...purely platonic...but they've been able to cultivate my natural leaning to be just a bit gutsy and independent. I'd be lost without my girlfriends, but it's sure nice to have the guys.

Programming

As my daughter's friend was explaining to me how he was programming my new word processor, it occurred to me that the love and support of special friends have been programming me for some kind of success right from the start of my singledom. I really don't feel very automatic these days. In fact, to the contrary, I melt very easily. This is funny because I'm starting to realize success in fields I never thought of, and having goals I never dreamed of before. I feel like my emotional walls or guards are coming down, and I wonder if this is good, because I could start feeling too many hurts this way. I still have many buried deep, but I'm afraid to think about what they are for fear of tearing myself apart. It's so much easier to keep busy, and whatever is going to come out will come out in due time. I can't spend the rest of my life looking for trouble.... It's just not productive. Now that I've started to reread the computer instruction book, I can't help thinking that it would be nice if we all came with books like this. It would save wear and tear on the psyche, if we knew what buttons to push...and why.

Depreciation

Everyone keeps telling me to stop depreciating myself. I guess it's a habit born out of being raised by a tough Jewish mother and an equally rough Jewish husband. Good manners were just one of the things that were on my mother's list. I can still feel the pinches and kicks under the table when we dined out. My husband was always trying to keep me in my place while he tried desperately to raise his brother, mother and two sons in and out of the family business he ran. Interestingly enough, both my mother and my husband were Scorpios. Although I'm really not into that stuff, in the future it might not be a bad idea to watch out for someone who's said to be a little more compatible with this easygoing Cancer. At least I used to be that way. In the last year and a half I have received more compliments than I've had in a lifetime. I have been called strong, capable, adorable and sweet, among other things. Referring to the way I took care of my ailing husband, a friend lived long enough, I would amount to something. She was trying to be funny, I think. It seems ridiculous when I'm still the same person that I was before, only now without a husband. Somehow put-downs from my friend give me that feeling of being somewhat normal again. I told him I was asked to be a model in a fashion show. He answered, "Who asked you, the Federation of the Blind?" He likes me! He likes me! I guess old habits are hard to break.

Leftovers

Most of the time lately I keep plugging along trying to keep my life spiced with new activities, or, at the very least, trying to keep up the old. I try to convince myself that there are some perks to living alone, and there are times it's rather soothing. But once in a while, when I have to deal with some of life's minor disappointments, not many, or if people say they're going to call and don't...then suddenly my insecurities reach a high level and tend to push away common sense. I then start thinking of myself as a leftover, and in a way I am. Leftover from a lifetime of emotional security and shared dreams with Dick. Even if a "Mr. Right" did come along, we could never have the same kind of dreams.... But then again, who says they couldn't be much better? There I go again, trying to pick up my spirits, just when I'm in the mood to be down.

Dollars and Sense

Pennies from Heaven

In the befores, my husband headed a national manufacturing company that featured a tree water tool. It was the family joke: "What do you think, money grows on trees?" Of course! At first my inheritance seemed to be pennies from heaven that Dick sent down to me. Needless to say, this situation had its perks, especially when the family business was sold and some of my "paper" turned into nickels. I soon realized that it had a down side, too, because I could no longer act like a dippy housewife. "I paid all the bills, honey, now fill 'er up again." Now I had to assume the role of a responsible, informed person, which was pure acting at the beginning, but the shoes are starting to fit. I hired a financial planner, not only to invest, but to keep me on a budget. Poor boy, he's paid in part just so I can bitch at him every month for not having enough money to blow. In any case, my favorite daydream nowadays takes place in a very fancy boardroom with an elegant me seated at the head of a very long conference table, flanked by a staff of damn lawyers, who all call me ma'am.

Well Provided

"Well, your husband left you well provided." He did, he did. And when did I stop saying, "Thank you, Dick," and when did I stop thinking of the money as his...it's mine!

L.A. Law

My surprised lawyer tells me it's starting to sound like "L.A. Law." The case that started out as a simple family injustice is blowing up like a balloon...with new deceits and conflicts of interest being discovered all the time. I have always felt that there is larceny in the best of families, so I could have lived with that for the sake of family unity. But even before Dick died, my sons and their wives were treating me like a second-class citizen. As a matter of fact, they weren't too nice to their father-boss, either. They must have realized that he was too sick to be of use to them anymore. But it was still a shock to see them turn into arrogant CEOs so soon after Dick died. When deceit was discovered and communication impossible, there was no other solution except the law to resolve a trust dispute. The "boys" threatened that if this case was not stopped, they would never let me see my grandchildren again. It wasn't the words, exactly, but how could children I had raised be so mean to their mother, or any human being, for that matter? Considering that they were measuring my visits anyway, I really didn't have much to lose. I begged for help from the rest of the family as well as the family lawyer, but to no avail. I was answered in many different ways, most often like "Gee, I get along with my family, that's too bad." I know that greed can show its ugly face when it comes to money, but never could I have imagined a scenario like this. For most of my married life, I was the one whom everyone leaned on, and now when I needed help, well, you know the story. One would have thought losing a husband would have been bad enough. I suppose the most frustrating thing was the way it forced easygoing Alice to grow up...like it or not.

Why Me?

I sit at my kitchen table downing one cup of coffee after another, trying to decide what is good for me, business-wise. Then for the first time ever, I hear myself saying, "Why me, Dick, why did you do this to me?" There have been more ramifications in the sale of the family business that have necessitated my finding yet another lawyer to check out my interests. In the past this scared me, but now I feel stronger. After a lifetime in which business and family members have been interwoven, some legal action could and probably would drive larger divisions in the family. Not to take these actions would prove I was weak. I've never been particularly materialistic, but I've never been alone before. Throwing emotional baggage out leaves me feeling so helplessly alone. I'm not scared...just lonely. When well-meaning friends have said, "If you don't take care of yourself, who will," I wonder if they have ever had to go through a process like this. I also wonder if this will make me seem hard boiled in the future. I realize now that even the process of thinking by myself is difficult, because in the past all I ever had to do was lean over and say, "What do you think, honey?" I can't even be concerned about that anymore because now, somewhat like my favorite daydream, I really am sitting at the head of a long table flanked by two attorneys, one investment counselor and one CPA. How about this! I've turned into a business commodity. I suppose this might be the time to end with "if only my friends could see me now," but this is no time to be flip.

Making Waves

"Don't you let them get to you. Don't you dare!" I hear my doctor saying in a very stern voice unlike his usual soft-spoken self. He's watching my blood pressure soar as I tell him what's going on with my children and the legal problems they're presenting to me. I look up and see the determined look on the face of this unusually sensitive man, and I can't help but realize this mess is making me tough, too. Gee, I miss my old problems. By the time this is over, I'll either have a stroke or be so tough no one will recognize me. Women in my generation weren't raised to make waves.... We just rolled along with the tide. With this new attitude, I'll never get a man.... You just wait and see.

The Crowd
Around Me

Family Ties

I have told so many people of the many ways my friends have shown kindness, that it was almost a surprise to think that was in the past. Now it's like a family of friends, and being included like this gives me a very special feeling. One of my closest confidants put it this way: "You're not dropping Dick's family, you just have our family, too." It's like moving out of town, or rather like being back in school, when I had the freedom to pick and choose whom I wanted to be with...and when.

Old Acquaintances

When the word got out after Dick's first surgery (implying serious illness), Christmas card names turned into concerned phone calls. They followed me through the bad years with lots of "You can do it!" This gave me much-needed strength as well as a link to the past. That was a miracle of sorts, because while they were concerned about my husband, I knew and they knew that I was uppermost in their thoughts. A slightly selfish part of me was comforted. Afterwards there were many little reunions around the country, and since they hadn't been with me in many years, they treated me almost like I was with them back in high school or college again. One of their husbands even thought it might be a good idea to contact some of the boyfriends I had back then, to see if their wives were dead. Shocking! Now a year and a half later, I miss the "Teenage Alice." But alas it was time to grow up again. However, in retrospect, this ol' gang of mine did what they set out to do. These very special human beings convinced me that I was special too, at least to them.

Making Lemonade

During the sick years, Dick and I always tried to squeeze every ounce of humor out of horrible circumstances. We made a lot of lemonade out of lemons those days. After he died I saw no reason not to continue coping in this manner. It always seemed to work for me. But when horror struck close friends of mine, somehow this method did not translate well. What do you say when a best friend's stepson persuades his dying father to leave practically everything to him, leaving the widow virtually penniless afterwards? How do you handle things when a fifty-five-year-old doctor is virtually imprisoned in a hospital room for two long months waiting for a new heart? And what is humorous about a close friend's beautiful thirty-five-year-old unmarried daughter having a mastectomy that the doctors are still nervous about? Fortunately, all these cases seem to be turning out okay, at least for now. But it wasn't because I was serving lemonade. In fact, it gave me a taste of what dear ones were probably going through when Dick was so sick. I guess everyone has to write her own story, and all friends can do is wait on the sidelines, letting her see they're there. What a helpless feeling! I guess that's why I'm so self-centered these days. I can only deal with me.

The Passive Traveler

Aside from visits to see my family and friends, most of my travels are of the passive nature. That is, if there are invitations to attend out-of-town weddings or the like with my friends, I'm there. Even if it's starting to get a little old hat, there's still fun involved. These jaunts tend to give me the extra bonding that I need to structure my new life now.

Wonder if they'd love me if I were poor. Too many more of these deals, and I will be.

It's in the Cards

Then there's my weekly card games where nothing, but nothing, is sacred. For the first time in my life I feel free to join in raucous fun. The use of four-letter words starting with "F" and "S" have more to do with hands dealt that natural urges...and this led me to tell them, "I know Dick is resting peacefully, because he left me enough to socialize with the genteel society, you know, the real swells in town." They stopped to listen for a minute, and then said, "Fuck off, Alice, and get back to the game!" It sure is fun being high class!

Part of the Game

After our card games are started and the nibbles are noticed and gobbled, there comes a time when the conversation turns to the home front. The current gossip is shared, new jokes are tried out and then the bitching starts. Most of it has to do with what to fix for their husbands' dinners. I listen and wonder why they don't remember my circumstances. I understand what they're saying, because I used to do the same thing. Maybe after three years they don't think of me as being different. Conversations like these continually remind me that I am.

A Caring Neighbor

A caring neighbor tells me she sees through my "sparkling eyes and fun demeanor," because she knows how very deeply I have been affected by family problems. This makes me wonder why I'm able to look and act this way; maybe this description should fit some kind of mental illness. I know I would like to think that maybe I just bounce back better than most.... But time will tell.

Good for You!

When I run into people whom I haven't seen for months (or years), they usually start the conversation by asking me how I'm doing. I've started to realize that no matter what I answer, their favorite reply is to give me a pat on the shoulder accompanied by "Good for you!" This phrase has been repeated lots lately. The very next time this happens, and it will, I would dearly love to retort, "Well, I'm rubbing out wives when their husbands interest me. You better watch out!" Don't tell me, I know. They will answer back, "Good for you!" I guess you can't listen with your mouth open.

The Eyes Have It

That summer when I was in Chicago visiting friends, I had a wonderful reunion with a very special lady who had moved to the area to be closer to her children. I had missed my dear elderly friend, whom I hadn't seen in eight months. She kept staring at me until she observed, "Your eyes tell me you are making fine progress."

"Even with tears in them," I answered. I hadn't thought of her words until recently when one of the husbands approached me and said, "There's something very different about you lately, and I've finally figured out what. It's your eyes, they're sparkling." I guess all the eye shadow in the world can't do a thing when you're dead inside.

Single

I wonder now just when the invitations stopped coming. It's been months since I've been included in an informal supper with married friends, and lately these weekends seem to last forever. So this is what they talk about when one feels dropped out of a social life. I'm remembered for the big galas, but somehow a spur-of-the-moment invite for a casual meal, in or out, is just for couples. Being single means I can't make the first move unless I'm hosting the evening. I have nothing against that either, but that would get stale after a while. Does this mean it's just women friends from now on? It wouldn't be the end of the world, but I couldn't take a steady diet of it. I start to remember in my "other life" when eating out alone meant just with the husband. I remember the advice I gave my daughter once, "Sometimes you're in the best company when you're by yourself," but then decide that's probably just a case of sour grapes. I guess even with all the efforts I've been making, one can't fight the system. Single is single is single!

Just a
Little Glitz

Rings on Her Fingers

From the beginning of our marriage, I swallowed Dick's lines such as:

"Valentines are only from husbands who are not nice to their wives the rest of the year."

"A fur coat would make you look like a teddy bear."

When I told him I was tired of junk jewelry, he replied, "Don't tell me you're turning into one of those kinds of women."

When I related the last statement to my mother (I had thought the remark funny), she quipped back, "I hope to hell you told him you were that kind of woman." I didn't because, crazy as it might seem, I really thought Dick was right. With this in mind, you can imagine how taken aback I was, right after his first surgery, to find out that he had made arrangements to get me a mink coat. (I should have realized his days were numbered.) Then he had daughter Suse help select a lovely cocktail ring for my birthday, when a new vacuum cleaner would have done the trick. And a month before he died, he insisted that I have my engagement ring reset in a wide gold band like the rest of my friends have. All of these generosities left me feeling somehow cheap or shallow. Did he feel that he had to somehow pay me for nursing care? I knew he felt guilty about what he was putting me through. I guess telling him honestly that to me it was part of "for better or worse" didn't register. He in turn explained that he never had the time before to reflect on the things he hadn't done and wished he had (God, he was sweet!). Then I started to feel that he was getting me ready for camp, or widowhood, as the case might be. What the well-dressed widow should be wearing. So taking a cue from him, I have been buying myself gold bracelets for each birthday, and this year a diamond-and-gold heart on a chain. (What kind of widow has a bare neck?) The gypsy song "for she has rings on her fingers and bells on her toes" comes to mind, but when you get right down to it, they are a very poor substitute for a loving husband. I guess in my heart I'll never be "that kind of woman."

Cutting Cords

During a recent trip to the east coast to see friends and relatives, I had a chance to distance myself from the home front. Somewhere in this time frame I finally took my wedding ring off. I had tried to do this several times before, but it never seemed right. Maybe it was the timing, or perhaps the adventure of travel itself made me finally feel "single." So I cut the cord, not to Dick, but rather to my married friends. Somehow my ringless finger makes it official that I'm not one of them anymore. I am alone. Have I been playing the role of a married lady? If so, it's even more important for me to find a single group, if only to balance the act somehow. In any case, I wonder how long it will take to fill in the pale ring on the empty fourth finger on my left hand. After twenty-three months, it's time to go public.

Little Red Dress

When I received one too many invitations, I finally decided it was time to buy a new cocktail dress. Luckily I was able to find the perfect one on sale, and though I never wear red, I bought it anyway. The money I saved on the sale was spent buying shoes, handbag, earrings and of course lipstick and nail polish. It was hard to find them all in matching shades of red, but I managed. I surprised myself since this is so out of character for the likes of me. The excitement grew, and I can't remember when I had so much fun. It had all the trimmings of going to my first prom. Trust me, I wasn't looking to attract a man, or even to gain compliments from women friends. It just felt good to play dress-up! The big evening finally arrived, and a special gal friend came over to assist me in getting dressed. I was a picture in red, and the thought occurred to me that I might be looking more like a gay divorcee than a merry widow. My friend made me promise that no matter what anyone said about the low cleavage, I would take it with a grain of salt, and not wisecrack like I usually do. It was long after I returned home that I realized that with all the compliments I received, no one had commented on the color. When you think of it, that must have meant that red brought out the best of me, and not vice versa. How about that for reflecting how I'm looking and acting these days?

Brotherly Advice

Once when my younger brother and I were still in our twenties, he told me what I really needed to jazz up my image was to hold a martini glass in my hand. "It could have just water in it," he said, "but it would give you that air of sophistication you so sorely need." He always was a smart ass! But I hate martinis, so I never did take his advice. I hadn't thought of this in years, until the other night. While dressing for the symphony, I suddenly realized that the only prop I need for the sake of image these days...is me.

Sexy at Sixty

My editor calls sounding embarrassed. He says, "Now don't get mad, but we're doing a series, 'Sexy at Sixty,' and I want to do a profile on you." Mad? My heart leaps excitedly as I answer, "Terrific. I'd love it. Does it make any difference that I'm not sixty yet?" Alas, it did, but what an upper when a younger guy that I respect thinks I'm a with-it type person. Actually I don't know what he was hesitant about, because he could have called me "sexy at eighty" as long as he spelled my name right. What's happening to me?

Ahhhh, Men

Platonic Relationships

The movie "When Harry Met Sally" was wrong when it implied that there's no such thing as a platonic relationship. I have such a friend. He comes to town a week after the funeral of his friend and business associate, my husband. He makes me get dressed up and takes me out to dinner (which is another story); he sends me a set of handkerchiefs with printed instructions on how to drop them to attract a man; he reminds me that returning hugs from the husbands for support is a good way to lose their wives as girlfriends, no matter how innocent it looks; and he makes me laugh deeply (sure felt good) with his teasing and horrid cartoons. Above all, he teaches me that unlike my super-strong husband, real men can indeed cry, hurt, have insecurities and are not ashamed to share these human frailties with close friends. This makes me realize it's okay for real women to feel this way too.

Dining Out

With my husband's friend and business associate waiting downstairs, I nervously try to select a dress suitable for dining out. I don't want to eat fancy, but he insists I deserve to be spoiled. It's Friday, and Dick has only been gone a little over a week. Why didn't I realize that when he said he was coming to town, this might be a problem in itself? Suddenly he's turning into a man and I'm acting like a schoolgirl. To add to the situation, my daughter decides she's coming home for the weekend and doesn't think I realize she plans on chaperoning. As we leave the house, I start to suggest places, but he's already made reservations at one of the chic new restaurants in town. It's been so long since I've been out to anything fancier than a fast-food place that I start wondering if I can remember what fork to use for each course. We're barely seated at a cozy table for two when, out of the corner of my eye, I notice a parade of familiar faces walking into the room. I gulp as I realize at least half the couples in this large crowd have been in my home the week before, paying sympathy calls. There are quite a few surprised glances toward our table. My friend notices, and then starts clowning around romantically in an attempt to calm me down. I take a deep breath and wait for visitors that never come. This of course makes the situation even more embarrassing. "They must think I'm a scarlet woman," I tell him. Looking back, I realize that they too had been put in a no-win situation. My usual common sense and good humor were being stretched to the breaking point. After a hectic evening which surprisingly turned out to be fun, we return home where the "kid" is already in town, waiting for us with one of her friends. She listens to the story we tell, and finally comments, "My mother, the slut!" Is that better than "scarlet woman?" I wonder. After he leaves, they reassure me that I had indeed done nothing to feel guilty about. "After all, Mom, he's not even a man, he's just an old friend." I smile to myself, not wanting to shock her by saying out loud, "No, my darling daughter, he's a man, all right, and quite a man." No matter what else had happened, that observation had not escaped my attention. My single thinking had begun.

Attitudes Like Mine

Three of the last four men that I have known as a single woman, alas still not in the biblical sense, have displayed certain personality traits that tend to puzzle me. I'm not sure whether it's their age group or what. They start by offering me travel opportunities, and then start subtracting five to ten years from their ages. I have told at least two of these so-called gentlemen to stop dangling trips in front of me as if I were a cocktail waitress. Don't they realize that at this point I could be had for a small bag of jelly beans, a funny card, or at the very most, an ice cream cone? Maybe this is nothing more than lines that single women are fed in the nineties. Where is the wisdom that should come with their age...or has women's lib destroyed any need for it? I know that as soon as I refuse to share their bed, there will be another to grab the opportunity. I guess I'm not as lonely as I think I am, but with an attitude like mine, I'll die a virgin yet; you just wait and see.

My Buddy

What is a good friend? Could it be a buddy with whom you find yourself complaining for hours that you miss having a man to talk to...and he never gets mad? In fact, somehow, he's always there to give me the right advice at the right time about absolutely anything and everything. He's very brilliant, talented and much younger than I am. This is a plus, because if he were my age, I might be tempted to think of him differently, and then I'd lose a real pal. I won't take his friendship for granted anymore, because special platonic men friends are few and far between. I'm lucky to have two of them. What a deal!

Taking a Chance

I was on the east coast visiting a widowed friend. One evening she showed me an ad in a prominent local magazine. It was from a matchmaker who promised that a thousand dollars would give an applicant three introductions to most eligible men. She had been out with a few "fixes" that had had funny, but unhappy endings (they didn't think she would notice that they couldn't perform) and was eager to meet a healthier specimen. Because I hadn't met anyone so far, I told her that if I lived closer, I myself would be tempted to join her in this endeavor. Apparently that gave her the courage to pick up the phone, and I held her hand as she nervously made the necessary arrangements. After returning home, I shared this story with my friend. He listened, then chuckled and said, "Hey Alice, I have a great idea. Why don't you offer to buy her rejects for half price?" We both laughed, but after hearing the results of her three dates, I doubt very much if I would have paid a nickel on the dollar for the opportunity. Who says money can buy happiness?

The Burgundy Olds

A few months before Dick died, my neighbor passed away from cancer. Her husband was very grateful to me for helping the family with some of the funeral arrangements. He in turn was very thoughtful when it was my time to be helped. He even had me stop over for coffee after some of my therapeutic walks. Time passed, and one day I thought I would reciprocate and invite him over to my house. I was a little nervous about it, but I figured it wouldn't hurt to pay back his hospitality. He apologized, saying he couldn't because he was involved with a woman. I was a little surprised because I felt it was so soon after his wife's death, but even then I couldn't figure out what that had to do with having coffee with a neighbor. I started wondering why the gods couldn't have been a little kinder about the type of widower that fate had put across the street from me. Would it have been so bad to have somebody who was a little more my type? In any case, shortly after this conversation, I started to see an old '70-something burgundy Olds parked across the street on the weekends, and the weekends grew longer and longer. A couple of months later he stopped over to bring me some homegrown tomatoes and suggested that I too could have a friend. All I had to do was to go bar-hopping like he did. "Loosen up!" he said. Boy, did he have the wrong gal. I laugh about the situation, but every time I think I'm doing okay—because I am—I see the car across the street. It sends signals to me that my life is still incomplete, and a feeling of unfairness sweeps over me. I wonder if somehow I will ever find a special visitor who will keep me company from time to time. Hopefully the car in my driveway will be a Rolls.

Just One of Those Things

About a month ago, a girlfriend from a neighboring city sent me a personal column from her Jewish newspaper. She says it's time for me to start looking for a nice man, and knows it won't be in my city. The demographics are just not here. One ad seemed especially interesting. So I took heart in hand and answered. And then there was Tom (the name has been changed to protect the guilty). He had lost his wife in an accident four years before, and was looking to begin life again. Our personalities clicked almost at once. We started talking via the phone every day, sometimes twice. He had only taken his ring off a year before, but shyness and fear of disease had prevented him from any relationship. Without ever seeing each other in person, he claimed my personality and humor had turned him on, and he proceeded to talk in such a manner that I was tempted to get a 900 number. I should have been shocked by the situation, but it reminded me that though I had only been with one man, I did understand the male animal, or at least remembered him well. After our pictures were exchanged, I was amazed to discover how very much he resembled Dick. His loving talk made me feel like a real woman.... I guess being a wife just assures you of being female. Well, the lady's head was turned, but good. But then I started worrying about him being a fortune hunter, worrying about him persuading me to marry him when I wasn't ready, and in general worrying about everything except what I should have noticed. He seemed afraid to have a relationship in the flesh, and unfortunately I was not a sex therapist. The situation came to a head when I realized that I deserved better than "better than nothing." When last he called, I told him it was great fun, but it was just one of those things. He told me he would always love me, but he suspected that I would need someone who would stimulate me from the brain down, and not from the bottom up. I thought at the time that maybe that's the main difference between men and women to begin with. I thanked him for reminding me that I was not a girl but a grown-up woman, as well as for our wonderful mini phone romance. I miss him, darn it. Not only had he seemed like such a doll, but it had been wonderful feeling loved again. Damn! Damn! Damn!

More Great Fun

I could have sworn at the time it was over, but I would call him every couple of months just to hear his voice and to see if he had met anyone. After a couple of times when he said he was coming and didn't, he finally arrived at my front door. While he looked much older than his picture (like ten to fifteen years) he was nevertheless ruggedly handsome, and his warm and friendly charm just flooded the place. We hugged and talked, and although I told him I never did anything serious standing up, it was very tempting. He was visibly upset that we didn't start something five minutes after he arrived. We had just returned from a lovely walk around my neighborhood and were getting ready to leave for a late dinner when his eighty-seven-year-old mother, whom he lived with, called to tell him that she had fallen and hurt her ankle. Would he come home and take her to the doctor? Just how stupid did he think I was! I realized he must have called her when I was upstairs. He really must have been disappointed in my attitude to make up this kind of story. We stared at each other in a state of shock, but to my surprise I felt almost relieved. I told him he must get back in the car and help her (and we're talking three hundred miles now). Before he left he grabbed me and did a quick manual check of what he thought he was going to miss, and I surprised myself by returning the favor (so how's that for women's lib?). He looked so sad that I said, "It was just one of those things," to which he answered, "Yes, but it was great fun."

More Lemonade

My world seems to be falling apart. My friendship with Mr. Great Fun has crumbled, and while I knew in my heart something was not kosher about the gentleman, he did almost charm the pants off me. But I suppose that's because I'm now what they call a vulnerable widow. I keep trying to milk the good things out of this experience, and there are many. He kept calling me "beautiful and sexy," and somehow for the first time in my life I realized that you don't have to be tall and lanky to be attractive to men. The funny thing is that I keep forgetting that Dick was an extremely handsome six-footer, and needless to say he had no problem with my looks. But this is today, and people who see me all the time are saying that I look beautiful lately, and I'm not even tempted to ask, "Who, me?" I suppose the biggest favor was making me realize that, with the right guy, I think I might be willing to share again. What a lovely gift that is. See, I've made lemonade out of lemons again, and if I weren't feeling so lost these days, I'd be tempted to drop him a thank-you note.

The Printed
Word

Windows Open When a Door Is Closed

In the beginning I kept hearing the saying "Windows do open when a door is closed," but I really didn't see how this could apply to me. But now I've turned into a believer. Sharing a Sunday night supper with friends, our hostess announced that she had taken over the editing and re-vamping of our little Jewish Federation newspaper. "And furthermore, Alice is going to write a newsy little column." After I stopped choking on the food in my mouth, I was able to say, "That's a wonderful idea, but I don't write...never have." "That's okay," she answered, "you'll figure something out." Driving home, I decided that since this was her idea of therapy, I could at least tell her I tried. Hours later, with pen, paper and a collection of synagogue bulletins (after the column was established, readers would call me with news) I started to jot down some information that she had requested. And then, as if I were thinking out loud, thoughts poured onto the paper, and I had my first column done in less than ten minutes. I have been writing one every month since, and everyone seems to enjoy seeing their names in print as well as reading my thoughts on different subjects. Amazing! People seek me out whenever they see me, and usually start the conversation with, "I didn't know you could write," and I quip back, "I didn't know I could either." Ain't fate grand! "Windows do open when a door is closed."

Letter to a Friend

Hi, it's me again, and it's sure fun feeling electronic. I never in a million years thought I would be having so much fun with this word processor. I guess I've been dragged screaming and kicking into the twenty-first century, and the whole process is once again adding to the persona of yours truly. Why did I ever think that I was too plain to fit in with the fast pace of today's world? Of course I can do it...I can do it...I can do it. And one reason is that you knew I could. Thanks for always giving me confidence (in some areas). Wouldn't it be a kick if I turned into the very thing that Dick always bitched about...a computer nut!

Ask Alice

Someone suggested that I should talk to the editor of a local paper in town to see if they could also use me as a columnist. So with my new self-confidence I made an appointment and showed him what I had been doing. "I really don't know if what I'm doing is good writing," I said, "I just know that people enjoy seeing their names in print." Apparently he gleaned some talent, and thought he had a perfect project that might be right up my alley. Because the holiday season was upon us, he felt the paper could use an in-depth article on Chanukah and how it's celebrated in a small Jewish community. Of course I can tap dance, I thought, but I smiled confidently and committed myself to the project. To this day, I have never worked so hard on anything in my life. This was a real article, not just a simple column. It proved to be quite a hit, but then the editor told me that though he had nothing else for me at this time, he would keep me in mind for something in the future. "If you come up with a project, call me." Three months later, I still hadn't heard from him, and I was pretty down. During a phone conversation with my friend, I complained about the situation, wondering what to do next. "What about being an advice columnist?" he said. "You're crazy! I don't have any credentials for that type of work." He laughed, "Neither did a couple of twins we know." Leave it to him! But the very next morning I thought, "What the hell," and made the call, saying nervously, "Can you use an advice columnist?" His quick answer surprised me, "Sounds good to me. Let's call it 'Ask Alice.'" So much for pounding the pavement. I don't know what I was concerned about, because like everyone else I know, giving advice is easy.... It's the taking it that can be difficult sometimes.

A Letter to Another Friend

The White House
Dear Barbara Bush,
Your commencement address at Wellesley spoke to me. I am a fifty-six-year-old "mermaid" who lost her husband almost two years ago after thirty-five years of marriage. At the time I was left feeling like half a person, until a "window" opened and I discovered a writing talent I did not know I had. Now, two columns later, with notes for a book, I have a dream, too. Your directives have thrilled me; I know you're our first lady...but you have become a friend in need. Thank you.
Most sincerely,
Alice Daniels

The "mermaid" reference was to a girl who listened to a different drummer. Her address was dedicated to all the "mermaids" in the world.

Mixed Blessings

How's this for heartwarming? My newspaper editor reads my tear-stained vignette on unrequited love, shakes his head and says, "I'm really sorry about all of this, but it's great writing, keep it up!" He also implies he's going to line up a group of gents to keep breaking my heart for the further development of my writing skills. Oh, cruel world, where does it say in the writer's manual that I have to be celibate to be good? Maybe it's time to switch to acting.

Stop the Presses!

My editor never intended to manage, he just wanted to write. It never occurred to me to write, I just wanted to cope. But this super-sharp young man and I agree on so many things that I can't help wondering if I'm super-sharp, too. What a lovely thought to chew on!

Famous Local Columnist

I agreed to speak as part of a panel at my Temple Sisterhood. Receiving the announcement, I was shocked to see myself described as "Famous Local Columnist." Actually, shocked wasn't the word. It was more like embarrassed. I waited for teasing phone calls from my friends, which never materialized. When the subject was mentioned casually, it was only to reflect on how darling the publicity was. I called my friend and told him how I felt. "I keep telling you, you're a celebrity," he said. "That's nonsense," I replied. "We're talking a couple of little papers in my home town...and besides, the writing does me more good that anyone else." "Alice, it's not how you feel, it's how people perceive you." I thought about this for a long time after we hung up, and realized he might be right. Boy, that's a relief. Acting famous would be too much of an effort for me at this time.

You're Something Else

A new friend calls to say he just finished reading the latest "Ask Alice" column and has a problem comparing the logical answers with the crazy lady he knows in person. I repeat this comment to one of the girls, who giggles, then says, "Well, he's just beginning to know what we all see in you. You're really something else!" Well, you can't be logical all the time!

Thank Yous

While talking to my "Harry and Sally" friend last month, I asked him point blank a question that has been bothering me for a long time. With all my surprising writing talents emerging, I found more self-confidence, and I finally got the nerve to ask out loud, "Do I thank Dick for dying so that I could find myself?" Needless to say, there was a long pause before he answered, "Don't be silly." His words for once did not satisfy me. You have to admit that this kind of thinking is creepy, honest or not. But when I asked my buddy, his answer made sense. "No, Alice, you thank Dick for leaving you in a financially secure situation so that you are free to explore all opportunities as they present themselves." Obviously friends like that are to be thanked, too.

More Titles

Now that my mind and writing hand are stretching into more than my column, I find that "widow," "Alice," "Gramma" and/or "single" are somehow just not me anymore. I am now known as an "advice columnist" in a local newspaper, and at least two of my friends are starting to call me "Grandma Moses." This is a mixed blessing considering what I pay my hairdresser for color. But my friend (bless his heart) has suggested that "Boom Boom" is more descriptive than "Moses," and it certainly has a ring to it. I like "Boom Boom!" It's so apt.

Widows and
Widowers

It's Okay

I suppose married friends wonder how I've adjusted to being alone. I hope they'll never have to experience this, but when and if their time does come, I'll probably tell them what I've discovered. It's not what you can't do when you think your life is over, it's what you can do. It's okay to giggle (preferably not at the funeral); worry about how you look; tell jokes; rejoin the social world (such as it is); relocate if necessary; and, heaven help us, even notice the opposite sex. That's the funny thing about being widowed. Whether you do these things or not, it doesn't seem to change whatever it is that makes one feel like half a person sometimes. I had the occasion to tell someone recently that I suspect when two widowed people marry, there are really four people at the altar, not two. "They" are always with us. In time, these emotions will adjust to their own level and allow the freedom and joy of new beginnings. Occasional flare-ups can occur, but these can be handled too. Eventually everything turns out okay; maybe not perfect, but okay.

Cancer Widow

My young thirty-something neighbor passed away, leaving a lovely wife and two small children. Although we hadn't been close, I went over to see what I could do for her. She had just returned from a major medical center where they had tried a last-ditch effort at a marrow transplant. "Cancer widows" are a breed of their own, because I recognized immediately her upbeat attitude, even though she looked like hell. As we hugged each other, I heard myself saying, "Your eyes look familiar," and she responded, "You know, my God, you know!"

The Cope Group

This sounds almost weird. Now that I finally have established myself as single and not just a widow, I have joined a cope group for widowed people. My darling young neighbor has been urging me for months to go with her, and I kept saying that I'm past needing this stuff after more than two and a half years. She finally had her way, and I went, feeling both cynical and just a little curious. But when I started sharing within the group, I found myself crying when asked a natural question, "Can you tell us about the moment your husband actually died?" Apparently I had missed a beat somewhere along the line, because it felt so surprisingly good to be able to share these deep feelings and thoughts with people who understood, instead of talking to myself or to the word processor. After the first several months of widowhood, I always tried to control myself in public, feeling that nobody likes a cry baby. Besides, everyone always expects me to be upbeat all the time. Now, in this group it's okay to let it all hang out. Aside from monthly meetings, those who wish are invited to eat together each Wednesday evening at one of the local restaurants. I can't help but remember all the meals I have eaten out by myself. The women far outnumber the men, but somehow it doesn't matter, because the warmth and caring that I experience are so very special. Maybe I couldn't participate in a group like this before because I felt that I was better than average and didn't need "crutches" like other widows do. What a relief to have the best of both worlds now...and to discover that it's not so bad being normal.

Newly Wounded

Looking around at one of the "widowed people parties," I couldn't help but notice the faces of the newly wounded. The eyes of the women were blank, but the eyes of the men showed so much pain and hurt that I had to turn away. "Why the difference?" I ask myself. Maybe women are programmed for these life-cycle events, while men have been told they'll never outlive their wives. They are in a state of shock and surprise. Come to think of it, why am I at the word processor instead of in the kitchen making casseroles for the poor dears? Guess I'm not that desperate yet.

Ass Backward

I keep thinking about how satisfying my first visit to the cope group was. Most people couldn't have gone on with their lives without this type of support to get them going. The fact that I seemingly got along without it means that I was missing something in the grieving process. So with my natural aptitude for doing things ass backward, I had to fight things out myself, and then get help. It also occurs to me that my wonderful friend, who guided me back into the world of the living, is a product of divorce. Would my lifestyle have been different if he had been widowed? Only the shadow knows!

Invisible

A widowed friend from Philadelphia says that "all widows are invisible. After a while, not only men but everyone ceases to notice we're around." I'll buy that! They probably realize that they're only a heartbeat away from being one of us, and that alone is not a pretty sight.

Books on Widowhood

While I've never felt that books have all the answers, I'm aware that they're out there if I need them. One just has to watch the talk shows to see authors discuss every problem imaginable. I was advised to read the book *Widow*, but I saw the television movie instead. It starred Michael Learned. I couldn't relate, because I figured this stuff was for lonely ladies who were talented, slim and looked like Mother Walton. Actually, if the truth were known, I've always felt, and still do feel, that every person writes her (his) own book, so it's hard to generalize. I know instinctively what the books would tell me, but as you might have guessed by now, I have to do things my way...for better or worse.

Woes of Some Widowers

Where there's smoke there's fire, so I assume the two widowers I'll tell you about are not isolated cases, just ones who have affected me personally. There's the one who lost his wife three months before Dick died, and one who was just recently left alone. I was rather close to both wives, so it was understandable that both men feel close enough to me to share these intimate feelings. It seems that both have found "lady loves" within six months after the funerals, and though they make it quite apparent they'll never marry again, they seem quite happy to have some of the creature comforts the cats fight over. But what is there about me, I ask, that they feel they must keep crying on my shoulder about how they keep visiting the cemetery and going into depression on special anniversaries? I keep telling the gentlemen that one thing doesn't necessarily have to do with another, but it doesn't seem to soothe their consciences. I wonder why they think I'm an expert on this situation. I guess getting a blessing from a friend of their wives somehow means their wives would have approved of their situation, too. I wonder if it ever occurs to these egotistical giants that I'm alone, too. Given the same set of circumstances, would widows feel the same? But then again, widows should be so lucky.

Odds 'n' Ends

Holiday Season

I guess it's true what I've heard about the holiday season. It certainly can be a nesting ground for depressed thoughts. This is the first time it's happened to me, and that's surprising because I've had better reason for it in seasons past. In spite of some turmoil in my life, I'm finally beginning to see light at the end of the rainbow. My financial planner has told me I can do what I want, as long as I "don't act crazy"; my daughter is finally on her way up in the business world; the invitation list for my New Year's Eve party has names on it I hadn't even heard of last year; and I'm finally starting to earn the love and respect of the darling men and women who seem to add such structure to my life. I do realize, though, that at the core of my problems is the knowledge that while I've grown so far away from my other life, I do miss my sons. Why am I so surprised that these honest truths are finally surfacing? Of course I miss them! Sadly, I think we've gone too far for this situation to be reversed. I consider this a trade-off for finally coming to my senses and seeing things the way they are instead of as I wanted them to be. The clock is moving slowly.... But this season will also pass. Hopefully blessed normalcy will return soon after that.

Three-Year Cycles

My interest span has always seemed to run in three-year cycles. As I approach the three-year anniversary of Dick's death (it's still hard to see these two words in print), I wonder what new things will be in store for me in the next three years. One thing for sure. I've started a deliberate attempt to separate myself from the emotional attachment to my "Harry and Sally" friend in Chicago. He has been invaluable to my recovery, but the situation's going nowhere and I find myself comparing him to other men I meet, when I should be comparing them to Dick. Now isn't that interesting? He's almost like my teddy bear. I have to touch base with him every couple of weeks just for my own stability. I pretty well know what his answer will be when I ask the questions, but I have to ask for advice anyway. It's time to pull away, because he's been a tie to the past, and I look to the future. Hope I'm ready for this move. It feels scary as hell; but it's time!

When I Least Expect It

I had all but moved to Chicago to be close to my daughter. The house was all but sold, I was just starting to have second thoughts about the whole deal. I attended a holiday party that night just to make an appearance. I turned a corner (both literally and figuratively) and ran into a man whom I hadn't seen in over thirty years. I remembered he was divorced because I was used to running into his ex-wife. But for some reason this adorable man had only been a shadow in my past life. Boy was I a dummy! He started to talk, and talk, and I wondered how in the world had I missed him in this small community. Suddenly, as I observed him, I got this weird feeling ("Oh, m'gosh, it's him, you know, the one my friends keep saying that I'll meet when I least expect it"). I heard him saying, "It's fate! It's fate!" and I finally said, "It sure is fate. I'm moving to Chicago!" He didn't comment except to keep staring at me with a knowing grin. So who needs Chicago, anyway!

New Year's Eve

My first New Year's Eve alone was about six months after Dick died. I was in enough control of the situation to accept several New Year's Eve invitations to friends' homes. I thought that keeping myself busy was better than feeling sorry for myself at home. I drove my own car so that I had means to leave when I wanted. Actually, I was home before midnight just in time to avoid sad faces looking at me before the stroke of midnight. In December of the following year, I decided that to have a party at my house would leave me more in control of the evening. Actually the idea had begun a few years before, when I didn't like the idea of Dick being out in bad weather. This gave me the chance to surround him with those he loved in his own home. He loved it! Could I carry it off without him? Thinking about it, I realized that I was the one who actually did all the planning and cooking, and Ursula would help bartend as she had done years before anyway. I went ahead with the plan, sending out invitations, "Keep Me Company," and about eighty showed up. Though friends were awed at my bravery, things went quite smoothly. People came to the open house starting at 6:30, and by 9:30 the crowds had left for other gatherings. It was really a smooth deal. I did my once-a-year duty as hostess; it solved the holiday problem; my party was considered by many to be a payback, and so I was included in other festive occasions; and best of all I could again celebrate alone at the stroke of midnight without well-meaning friends nagging me. Way before "year four," I started hearing that I could never change this custom because friends loved the tradition. I had made the usual plans for the next one, which was now growing in size, but nevertheless routine...except for one detail. That detail was the fact that I had re-met an old friend two days before, at another party, and informally asked him to drop by on the thirty-first. I could have been alone at midnight, because everyone else had left at least an hour before...except him. The clock struck twelve (he showed me his watch), and I enjoyed a lovely kiss to start the new year. Can't help but wonder what other surprises await me.

Surprise

Now that I'm starting to feel secure in this new relationship, I find my closest confidants are not one hundred percent happy about it. They remind me constantly that he's not Dick. They seem on edge when I start to talk about the gentleman in question, and then there is silence. All this has been causing discomfort. Everyone else is excited that I have found someone to make me happy. I realize all too well that it's too soon to know the ending, but I can't think that far ahead. I finally got the nerve to ask someone what the problem was, and her answer (which I guess was reflective of the others) was to admit her jealousy of the addition to my life. I think, "How can people be so selfish? I thought they cared about my happiness." Later I shared these discoveries with my daughter. She claims that they don't mean to be selfish, but are fighting change. "They want you to be there for them, and they're afraid your new friend will somehow take you away." I start to wonder if she feels the same way, too. I feel terribly let down by their possessiveness because I was just beginning to think I understood people, and now this. I wonder if they want me down so they can feel better about themselves. In any case, it's a surprise!

Class Consciousness

The boyfriend keeps telling me that I'm much too classy for him. It's almost like he's trying to push me upstairs. It's sort of ironic because Dick was always putting me down, inferring that his background was better than mine, and now this guy is telling me the reverse. Wouldn't it be nice if I found someone who liked me just the way I am...right in the middle somewhere. Why does everything have to be so complicated?

Now I'm a Soap Opera

The three-year anniversary has passed. I'm still taping my soaps, but barely have time to watch them. Sometimes I think that I'm turning into a soap opera of my own, without a sponsor yet. There's always something new going on. If it's not legal problems, meeting writing deadlines or missing the grandchildren, then it's possible confrontations with my sons. My daughter is really in love this time, bringing thoughts of Dick, because I know how much he dreamed of this moment. My new friend is constantly testing me to see if I would make a perfect wife. That's driving me nuts, because I've already been through the perfect wife bit. Maybe I need some kind of biographer to keep track and record what I'm going through, because I sure can't. For the last few years I've been an observer of the human condition, and it's hard to be a participant again. Is this the normalcy I prayed for way back in the beginning? In any case, stay tuned, same time, same station. Looks like this book will never be finished.

Epilogue

A Man of Spirit

I'm still trying to tell you about Dick, and suddenly I remember words he shared with me only ten days before he died. I hadn't thought of this conversation until months afterward, but it was so special that I wrote it down and read it at the unveiling of his tombstone, which took place eleven months after the funeral. This should help explain why this bigger-than-life guy left a bigger-than-life gap to fill.

"Hey Al, I've been thinking.... I'm a lucky guy! Don't laugh, I'm not kidding. Obviously neither one of us needed the last two to three years, but when you think of it, I have a wonderful family and wonderful friends. I've built a business, and when it started to crumble, I was able to rebuild it too. I have three wonderful kids...well, just a few minor aggravations. But when you look around and see some of the heartaches other parents have, I wouldn't trade. I've had the love and support of a good woman, and now I've lived to see two beautiful grandchildren born. Yessiree, I'm a lucky guy!"

It's hard for those left behind to feel this way, but the more time passes, the more one realizes that at fifty-eight, Dick died believing he was lucky, and I guess that made him so. A man with spirit like this must be remembered in these writings. His strength must have been contagious.

Thank You, Darling

I'm starting to regress. I wish that sometime during our marriage I had told Dick just how much I appreciated him choosing me to be his friend, confidant, wife, lover and mother of his children. Remembering what a perfectionist he was, this really was quite a compliment. Maybe he was more special than I thought, because if you think about it, the "Root Feeder King" probably had been nourishing me at the roots all along, so that I could flourish in any situation. Thank you, Darling!